Summer
Exhibition
Illustrated
2012

A Selection from the 244th Summer Exhibition
Edited by Tess Jaray RA

Summer Exhibition Illustrated 2012

SPONSORED BY

Insight
INVESTMENT
➤ A BNY MELLON COMPANY℠

Royal Academy of Arts

Contents

Sponsor's Foreword

Insight Investment is proud to continue its association with the Royal Academy of Arts, a partnership that reflects values shared by both institutions: quality and creative thinking.

The Royal Academy strives continually to interest its visitors with thought-provoking works of art that stimulate their imaginations. Insight's focus is on providing clients with innovative solutions to meet their evolving investment needs.

Launched in 2002, Insight is responsible for £170 billion* in assets under management for a wide range of investors, including pension funds, corporates, sovereign wealth funds, insurers and private individuals. Our philosophy is to deliver consistent and repeatable performance for our clients through focusing only on doing those things we can do well. This has allowed us to build a reputation for excellence in liability risk management, fixed income, multi-asset and absolute return investments.

This year, our seventh as lead sponsor of the Royal Academy's Summer Exhibition, is a very special year. As the eyes of the world turn on London as it celebrates The Queen's Diamond Jubilee and the Olympic Games, the Summer Exhibition is showcasing contemporary British art alongside a large number of works submitted from overseas.

We hope that all visitors to the Summer Exhibition, together with Insight's clients, business partners and colleagues, will share our passion and find inspiration in the talent and creativity on display.

Abdallah Nauphal
Chief Executive Officer

* Insight's assets under management are represented by the value of physical securities and present value of liabilities subject to hedging strategies.

Introduction
Tess Jaray RA

Tess Jaray RA, the co-ordinator
of the 2012 Summer Exhibition,
selecting works from the
submitted entries.

The Royal Academy Summer Exhibition is notoriously demanding to take in, above all because of the sheer diversity of the work it shows. But it provides a unique opportunity to present emerging ideas and issues that concern artists today. Ideally this exhibition would comprehensively represent the best art being made across the world. Art at the moment is in excellent health, but there is not enough space, even in these large and wonderful galleries, to show it all.

There is no single theme for this year's Summer Exhibition. This is so that we may better reflect the diversity of subjects that artists are working with. We hope to clarify, not to explain. It is an exhibition designed to show some of the best British art currently being produced, within an international context. Or, it could be put the other way: a large number of international works shown within a British context. There are layers of expression running through the exhibition that may be gradually unravelled, elucidating these matters.

The work in the Annenberg Courtyard reveals one of these themes: that of the similarities and differences between art and architecture. This monumental object by Chris Wilkinson OBE RA, which is simultaneously an architectural installation, an exemplary piece of British engineering and a seat, perfectly expresses this relationship. A site-specific work, displaying great economy of means, it is both complex and rich in narrative and expression, and clearly refers to painting: its series of eleven frames (ten spaces) rotate through 90 degrees, each with a nine-degree shift, from landscape to portrait. This approach exemplifies how art and architecture in this country are starting to co-exist in a way that is new to this generation of practitioners, who address the problems of specific architectural environments. In front of Burlington House Wilkinson presents a fascinating solution to the question of how to contrast the old and the new, within the geometry of the courtyard and the geometry of his work. The external element of the exhibition is unified with what lies inside.

The octagonal Wohl Central Hall, painted red, is intended to be a wave, perhaps a homage, to Matisse's *Red Studio*, which, as many will know, once hung in a gallery on Cork Street, and was then purchased by the Museum of Modern Art, New York, after the Royal Academy tried, unsuccessfully, to buy it. John Singer Sargent, an Academician one hundred years ago, once said that red was the only true colour to hang paintings on. Here we have hung paintings that take colour as their main concern.

In Gallery III we emphasise the importance and the strength of smaller works. We are very glad to be showing a large number of young and emerging artists for the first time at the Summer Exhibition. Here we see that the visual arts are going through an unusual period. Perhaps 'going through' rather than 'arriving at', because art is always on the move, always 'becoming', rarely arriving, and partly because it is now much clearer that this new generation has interests that are very different from those of their predecessors.

There are now, as there have always been, stars in the firmament, more international and more highly priced than ever before. These shining names seem to have remarkably little effect on what young artists actually do, privately, in their studios. Long-gone are the days when such artists as Picasso or Matisse or Pollock were dominant. Picasso's hold over his contemporaries, for instance, was so great that some even ended their lives in despair at not being able to escape his influence. Through periods of 'high style', such as Cubism or Futurism or American Abstraction, there were very few who managed to work successfully in opposition to what seemed like the common currency of art.

Today, the power of celebrity artists over the younger generation seems to have waned. These young painters and sculptors and photographers and video-makers have somehow managed to free themselves, in their work, from glamorous ideas, and are now working straight from the heart.

There is, at the moment, a remarkable freedom of stylistic expression among young artists (in spite of a crisis of confidence in democracy). This is sometimes called 'pluralism', but 'freedom' expresses more clearly what is happening. Although some subject-matter reflects our universal problems, never before has art – visual art – been so private, so personal, so self-sufficient as it is now.

These young artists make work, mostly, it seems, about their lives; rarely about principles or ideals. If politics enters the arena, it is frequently in the form of installations, photos of wall-painted slogans, comic-strip extracts, or moments taken from television. Not many of this generation are making social protests or anti-war statements. It is as though the power of the individual voice to affect or change has been vanquished, as though there are no longer any honourable ways to work with ideals. Too much has been cheapened, kitschified. Young artists

have gone private, domestic, and perhaps, through this, are in some way rediscovering art's centre.

What subjects are these younger artists engaging with? Myriad: landscape, interiors, abstraction, the figure, geometry, fantasy. Paintings that study surface, or the meaning of a single colour, or the impact of a single form. Domestic subjects, subjects that refer to Western art history, and to the material of paint itself. No different, it might be said, from the subjects treated by artists over the past 150 years. Except that there is now a difference in the way they are put to use. Would any of the younger generation say, as Barnett Newman did in the 1940s, 'We are reasserting man's natural desire for the exalted.' Or, like Pollock, 'It doesn't make much difference how the paint is put on as long as something has been said. Technique is just a means of arriving at a statement.' Or, after Eva Hesse, 'I think art is a total thing. A total person giving a contribution. It is in essence a soul, and that's what it's about … In my inner soul art and life are inseparable…'

If you look at the works threading through this exhibition by artists from such countries as Iran or Iraq or Afghanistan, you see a very different aspiration, a very different view of the world. Hope, despair, conflict, urgency. If the subjects are domestic, they speak of loss and of pain, although through the very medium of art, by the mere fact that these are works of art – whether good or bad doesn't really seem to matter – they express hope. But in spite of the situation from which they emerge they do not seem to have the despair of Goya, or the fury of Picasso's *Guernica*. One cannot be certain why this is, but it is surely a reflection of the condition of the social worlds we live in. In art, contrary to general opinion, the world is perhaps not yet completely global.

In Gallery IV the majority of the exhibiting artists are Scottish and Irish, and painters in the traditional sense of the word, mostly trained in the Scottish art-college system, which places great stress on the importance of drawing and observational study. Some of the artists display this through emphasis on the human figure, some through landscape. The artists of international reputation and those that are included in the Summer Exhibition for the first time share these concerns.

In Galleries V, VI and VII, through painting to architecture to sculpture, we have taken on the challenge of presenting some of the shared precepts of art and architecture. Instead of categorising them by genre – landscape, urban, etcetera – we

are comparing the approaches of fine artists and architects to such concepts as space, form, material and structure. What does space mean to a painter, and what does it mean to an architect? It is used, and seen, very differently in each case. For example, the term 'structural imperative' is for architects a practical necessity but for fine artists it describes a necessity of a very different kind, that of the integrity of the picture plane, which anchors the work in space. Landscape, too, may be seen from opposing viewpoints, but with the same intention of using space for particular purposes. For architects landscape is a tool to an end, for an artist a tool for description or evocation. In both cases the same problem remains: how is space described?

Structure is central to both disciplines, but has varying significance: if the structure of a building fails, it has more practical – and disastrous – consequences than if it fails in a work of art. But for the artist, if the structure fails, so does the entire work. By blurring the boundaries between the disciplines, we are showing what links them together, rather than what keeps them apart. Not in order to explain, but to help to understand them in a fresh way.

Galleries VII and VIII show sculpture and demonstrate the affinities between sculpture and painting and architecture. From the *Venus of Willendorf* via Picasso's *Glass of Absinthe* to the present time, the small hand-held object can exert tremendous power out of all proportion to its size. In the 2012 Summer Exhibition the emphasis is on smaller works, and although, as always, space is at a premium, there are large sculptures to counteract any feeling of miniaturisation. Part of the great range of sculpture currently being made is displayed here.

Some works may jostle against each other; some are happily nudged into the category of architecture (as on another occasion architecture might be nudged into that of sculpture), while others will find sympathy with paintings. And there is much sculpture that stubbornly refuses to be anything but itself.

In a time of national belt-tightening those artists who use materials beyond the quotidian are up against it more than most – but in spite of hard times we are confident that sculpture in this year's exhibition will prove to be a celebration of what it is like to be alive now.

Galleries I and II show prints and drawings, with some photography. No longer do these media have to be separated from any others used by artists. Barriers have been broken;

there is no hierarchy now. Old and well-tried means of printing, such as etching or woodcuts, still hold their interest, and works made with these methods sit happily beside those in new and high-tech media. In these galleries it is interesting to see how today's printmakers have embraced the new technologies without abandoning the old. It is as though, by benefiting from the astonishing range of techniques now available, they have become more aware of the particular qualities inherent in the traditional ones. An etched line is like no other line in the world; the delicacy of a litho mark has not been superseded; but new kinds of paper and new kinds of inks have generated new kinds of work. The language of aesthetics always keeps pace with developments in technology.

Many artists are using print today because of its closeness to contemporary culture. Our world has been radically shaken by the digital revolution and this is a revolution that comes from, and shares many aspects of, printing. In many respects printmakers are involved in wider forms of communication. The multiple has democratic aspects, and artists who like the bigger arena can publish work that finds its way into many nooks and crannies as well as into the mainstream. There has been considerable interest in artists' books in the last few years. The more traditional print techniques are a sort of counter-culture that emphasises quality of production against the relentless commodifying drive of our time.

The installation in the Large Weston Room has been named 'Light and Earth'. Here there are works that refer to aspects of nature – to land, to growth, to dust and soil – to those things that seem to be basic, primal, fundamental, and to those things that shimmer, that illuminate, that reflect or gleam or radiate into the world. And sometimes to both. Works that seem to emerge from the earth into light. From night into day. There are works whose materials have been mined from the earth by the artist and shaped into something that belongs entirely to the light. Works in which trees are painted so close to nature that it is like being there, and which depict the transition from earth to light, and remind us of our own transience. And works whose aim is to be timeless.

Film is the chosen medium of many artists now, and we are showing it in the Small Weston Room, which is devoted entirely to the work of Jayne Parker. Parker is deeply interested in the way in which music is expressed, and in how the structure of

film may reflect the structure of music. In her films we see this through the various visual aspects of performance: the quality of a musician's concentration, the movement of his body, the touch of his hands on his instrument. Parker directs the viewer to hear the music in a different way. She articulates the experience visually, taking us 'inside' the performance in order to create something that touches our hearts, so that we really feel what we hear. She is asking: Where is music expressed? Where is the 'site of music'? Sometimes her films are intercut with images that symbolically or metaphorically lead us to think about the nature of music, of sound and the complex way it can affect us – that elusive quality that moves us, the mystery of the felt experience.

There is no single theme in Galleries IX and X, but the artists showing here express the vital and celebratory aspects of painting. These artists, many of whom are at the height of their achievements, rejoice in the world; they speak of pleasure and happiness; they remind us that the world is not merely full of problems and difficulties: that there is beauty and nature and fun and humour as well. That painting and music come from the same place, that love is a near relation, that in spite of much evidence to the contrary there is no law forbidding us to believe in the world, and to enjoy and celebrate it. They are saying: 'These things cannot be repressed. Life will assert itself.'

In the Lecture Room the work of Academicians and Honorary Academicians is exhibited, together with invited and submitted pieces. There is no particular theme here either; rather, the gallery shows some of the most established artists from within the Royal Academy and around the world, and the range of subjects and approaches that they use. Here one sees the great breadth of vision of art at this time. This gallery exemplifies, as does Gallery III, the freedom that artists have to express their individuality, not to feel bound to follow others. We have always known that art reflects the society in which it is made, and it is interesting to ask here: What does this art tell us about the world in its present state? And where is it telling us to go now?

The more mature artists in the exhibition demonstrate achievement, perseverance, stamina and force of will, as well as talent. But there is something else that runs throughout the show: the aspirational, yes, but also the intuitive and almost involuntary response of young artists to their society. Not thoughtless, but reflexive, immediate, and in some way, therefore, particularly true.

Left and above: selecting works for the 244th Summer Exhibition, including the 2012 Hanging Committee (centre) and Committee-member Humphrey Ocean RA (bottom left).

Tribute

Leonard Rosoman OBE RA

Peyton Skipwith

Selecting six works to represent the life of an artist who died a few months short of his 99th birthday is like choosing records for 'Desert Island Discs'. Leonard Rosoman first exhibited at Burlington House 70 years ago with the Fireman Artists, members of the Auxiliary Fire Service, and his stark *Burnt-out Fire Appliance* takes us back to that time, prior to his appointment as an official war artist. *A Bend in the Shrubbery*, a hauntingly empty landscape from the next decade, may depict the corner of a garden in Edinburgh, where Rosoman was teaching mural painting at the College of Art. His experience with mural painting and designing the Edinburgh Festival's 1954 Diaghilev exhibition, combined with his experiments with Rowney's newly developed acrylics, changed his manner of painting. John Osborne's play *A Patriot for Me*, set in the declining years of the Austro-Hungarian Empire and staged at the Royal Court Theatre in 1965, inspired Rosoman's largest series of paintings, including his Royal Academy Diploma Work, *The Promotion, No. 1*. The play's strange and disturbing situations influenced him, and the human figure, often in bizarre poses, came to dominate his work. The patrician Lord Esher, Principal of the Royal College of Art, where Rosoman taught in the 1960s, is the subject of one of his earliest discursive portraits, which embraces the setting as much as the person. The tilted landscape of Kensington Gardens, introduced as a painting within a painting – a typical Rosoman device – pays homage to those early Anglo-Dutch landscape painters commissioned to flaunt the extent of their patrons' estates.

Rosoman's habit of quiet observation and delight in the quirks of friends and fellow human beings come into full play in the two works most closely related to the Royal Academy: one a group portrait, the other a crowd scene. Older visitors to the Summer Exhibition will enjoy trying to identify the Academicians of yesteryear gathered round the committee-room table: Robert Buhler, Colin Hayes, Roger de Grey, Elisabeth Frink and Hugh Casson, among others. The figures milling around St Paul's Cathedral are no less real, but remain largely anonymous. The date of the painting, 29 November 1999, gives us the clue to the occasion: it was the day of Hugh Casson's memorial service.

The links that run through Leonard Rosoman's work are his unerring sense of pattern and his eye for the absurd: any little incident, perhaps only half-seen, could trigger his imagination and lead into unknown paths of exploration. At his funeral I quoted Wallace Stevens's lines:

> The man bent over his guitar,
> A shearsman of sorts. The day was green.
>
> They said, 'You have a blue guitar,
> You do not play things as they are.'
>
> The man replied, 'Things as they are
> Are changed upon the blue guitar.'

Leonard did not paint things as they were; he changed them into what they are.

Leonard Rosoman OBE RA
Portrait of Lord Esher, 1978
Acrylic
122 × 153 cm
Royal College of Art, London

Leonard Rosoman OBE RA
The Meeting, Royal Academy of Arts, 1979–84
Acrylic
152 × 152 cm
National Portrait Gallery, London

Tribute

John Hoyland RA

Mel Gooding

It is possible now to see John Hoyland's one-man exhibition at the Whitechapel Gallery in 1967 as a defining moment in British abstract painting. In his early thirties he had produced an astonishing body of work: huge paintings in which what he described as 'brilliant colour, full, unmixed … reds, greens and oranges' was deployed with an absolute formal clarity in radiant theatres of light. The intelligence, originality and imaginative grandeur of the paintings in that show established him as one of the two or three best abstract painters of his generation anywhere in the world.

Soon after, he travelled to New York: on his mettle, combative, keen to try himself in that competitive arena. But the blankly inexpressive surfaces, artificial colour and affectless 'cool' of American Post-painterly Abstraction failed to grip him. His own work became more painterly, more hectic and turbulent; he might have quoted his beloved John Constable RA: 'Painting is but another word for feeling.' Realising that he was essentially an expressive colourist in the European manner, Hoyland returned to England in 1973. *29.4.73*, with its four-square, impenetrable blocks of solid tonal reverberation, belongs to that period, in which he was finding his way back to the full-on colour that would characterise his painting for the rest of his life.

By the mid-1970s he had forged an intensely personal style in which strong forms, brilliant colours and complex textures were structured into compositions of a pulsating visual music, now a rich consonant chord, now a dissonance, now a harmony, now a discord. When these paintings were arrayed in sonorous grandeur at his 1979 retrospective at the Serpentine Gallery, it was clear that Hoyland was not only a colourist of genius, but also a master builder of 'great machines'. And like Constable's great Royal Academy 'six-footers', these are majestic orchestrations of the effects of nature into symphonic topographies. Hoyland's paintings of the 1970s might also properly remind us of Turner's tumultuous analogies, awesome painterly enactments of atmospheric natural process. Such paintings as *27.6.76* returned confidently to the English tradition of the landscape sublime. As Robert Motherwell, the American artist who best understood European painting, once declared to his friend, 'John, you could be the next Turner!'

John Hoyland RA
27.6.76
Acrylic
224 × 214 cm

Adrian Berg RA
Stourhead, 30 June 2003
Oil
131 × 187 cm

Tribute

Adrian Berg RA
Nick Tite

In the catalogue accompanying Adrian Berg's exhibition at the Serpentine Gallery in 1986, the influential – if controversial – critic Peter Fuller heralded Berg's landscapes as some of the most significant works dealing with the natural world to have been produced in the last quarter-century. Berg went on to have a number of gallery shows, yet by the time of his death in October 2011 they had all but dried up. Artists need galleries and critics to keep them in the public eye, and since Fuller's death in 1990 there have been too few championing Berg's cause. The memorial display in this year's Summer Exhibition serves as a reminder of the quality of Berg's work, but a proper survey is needed to assess his achievements and to see if Fuller's claim still holds water.

The paintings in this display depict typical Berg prospects. It so happens that these are Sheffield Park and Stourhead, but they could have been any of the great gardens of southeast England, to which Berg returned again and again, transforming cultivated nature into endlessly various celebrations of the changing seasons. These two oils are accompanied by two watercolours, one of the Alcázar in Seville (Berg's fascination with Islamic art informed so much of his art) and the other of Kew Gardens. Watercolour is a tricky medium but Berg slowly mastered it: the Lake District watercolours that he showed in the Sir Hugh Casson Room for Friends of the Royal Academy in 2009 (one of his last important exhibitions) came as a revelation to many who saw them. Produced on the spot, they had an immediacy and truth that captured the spirit of place.

Whether he worked in oil or watercolour, Berg tuned in to the evolving colours and forms of the natural world: the approach to the seasons of his friend David Hockney RA, as seen recently at the Academy, brought Berg to mind. And although his subjects ranged from landscape gardens and the Lake District to Beachy Head, it is probably for his paintings of Regent's Park that Berg will be best remembered. His almost daily engagement with the view from his studio in Gloucester Gate, where he lived and worked for some twenty years before moving to Hove in the late 1980s, produced his most pulsating images, full of discoveries and invention, canvases that explode with a Bonnard-like intensity. In some he used a grid format to represent the same scene at different times of the year, creating a sense of the passage of time, while in others he employed that same device to compose a panorama that sweeps the viewer through 180 degrees across the treetops and back again in giddy enjoyment. Berg's transformation of the natural world exudes the sensation of the perceived moment, a rare gift indeed.

Wohl Central Hall

Sonia Lawson RA
Postcard from Provence II
Oil
90 × 70 cm

Bernard Dunstan RA
Rehearsal – The Harp
Oil
26 × 31 cm

John Wragg RA
Waiting to Know
Acrylic
120 × 90 cm

Dr John Bellany CBE RA
Flowers
Oil
120 × 89 cm

Ian Davenport
Puddle Painting: Pale Lilac,
Yellow (After Bonnard)
Acrylic
200 × 200 cm

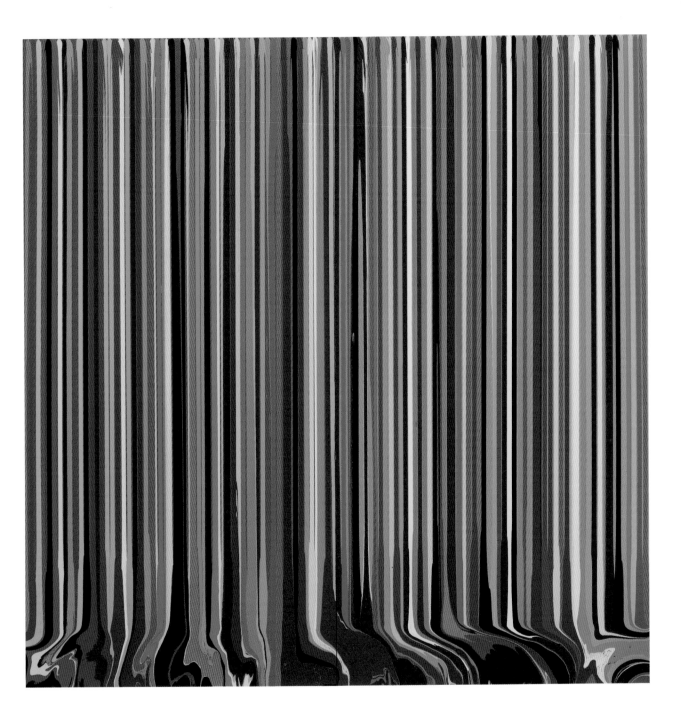

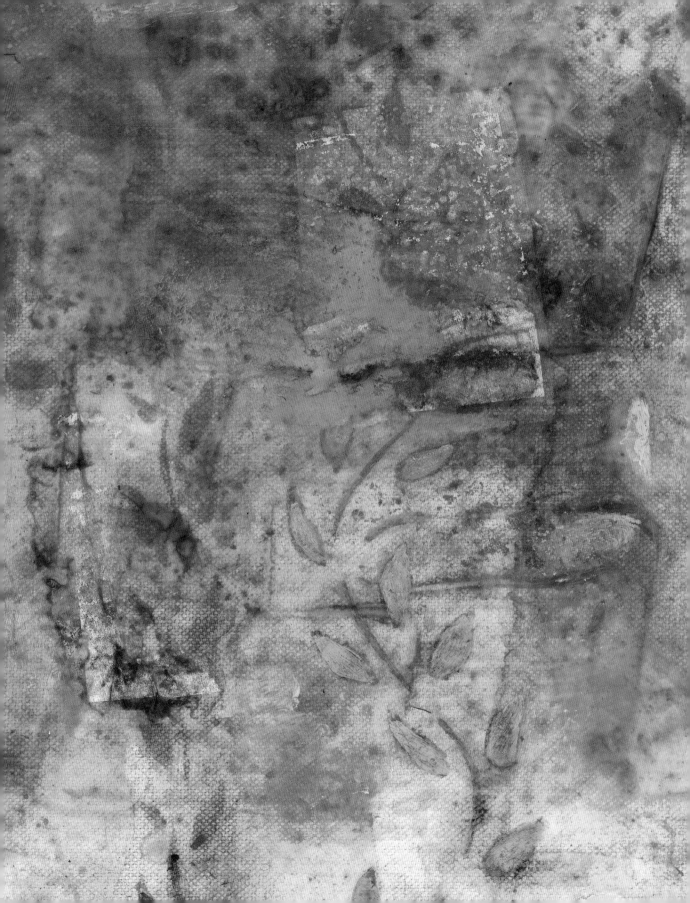

Mali Morris RA
Lost Light
Acrylic
25 × 30 cm

Tess Jaray RA
After Malevich
Mixed media
Diptych, each 30 × 30 cm

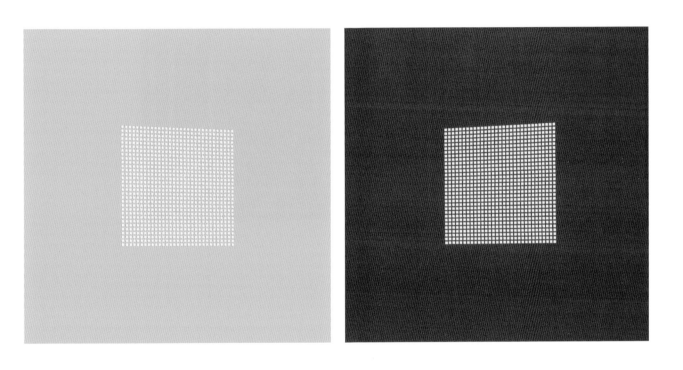

Neal Jones
The Hunt (After Uccello)
Oil on wood
64 × 100 cm

Dr David Tindle RA
Table
Egg tempera
31 × 42 cm

Deborah Burnstone
Quayside
Oil
30 × 40 cm

Hazel Leach-Evinson
Still-life in the Landscape
Acrylic
13 × 18 cm

Martin Creed
Work No. 1353
Oil
30 × 27 cm

Louis Nixon
Laurica
Acrylic
40 × 53 cm

Olly Fathers
Breeze Blocks
Acrylic
57 × 45 cm

David Small
Soft-corps
Mixed media
50 × 45 cm

Alex Hudson
Server
Oil
45 × 34 cm

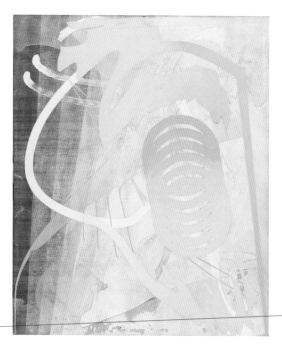

Gus Cummins RA
Off the Wall
Acrylic
54 × 75 cm

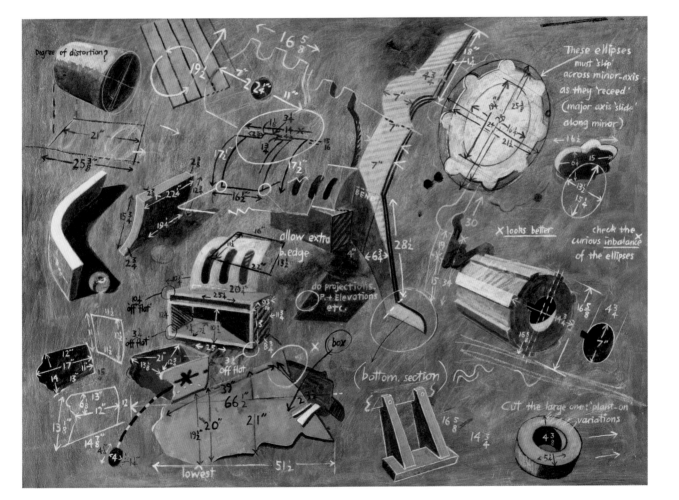

Dame Elizabeth Blackadder DBE RA
Japanese Plate with Fruit
Oil
47 × 55 cm

Mary Fedden OBE RA
Black Jug
Oil
34 × 35 cm

Andrzej Jackowski
Vigilant Dreamer
Oil
60 × 70 cm

Prof Stephen Farthing RA
Suddenly They Came into Focus, Voysey
Acrylic
71 × 71 cm

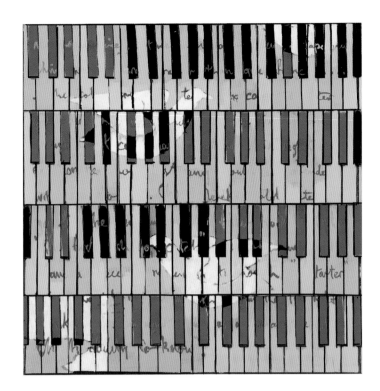

Ayman Baalbaki
Building F
Acrylic
35 × 27 cm

Andrea McLean
Meta
Oil
H 31 cm

Richard Kenton Webb
Listen – Orangeness
Mixed media
31 × 31 cm

Aman Mojadidi
Dressing for Work
(From 'A Day in the Life of a Jihadi Gangster' Series)
Digital print
85 × 55 cm

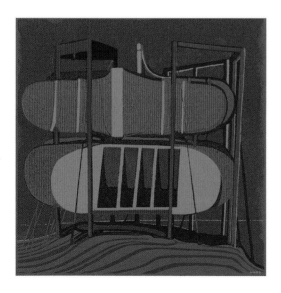

Olwyn Bowey RA
Miss Willmott's Ghost (Eryngium)
Oil
41 × 38 cm

Robin Lee-Hall
The Clever Young Man
Egg tempera
14 × 11 cm

Mick Rooney RA
Open-air Aviary
Gouache
41 × 31 cm

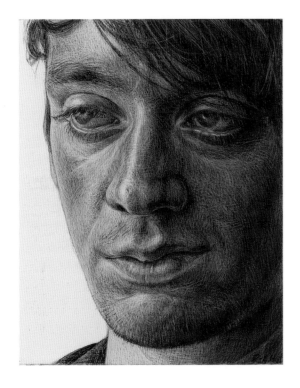

Basil Beattie RA
Head Rooms
Acrylic
40 × 50 cm

Alice Browne
LR
Oil
60 × 52 cm

Jane Harris
Yonder (Diptych) (detail)
Oil
51 × 122 cm

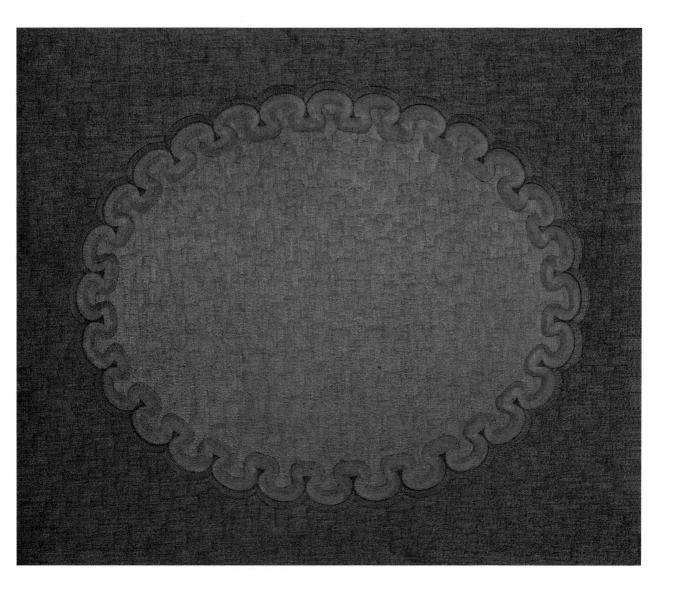

Phoebe Unwin
Paper and Street (Pair)
Mixed media
44 × 62 cm

Giulia Ricci
Order/Disruption Painting No. 1
Mixed media
36 × 36 cm

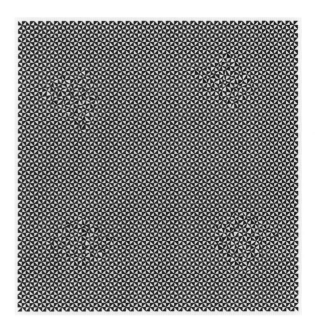

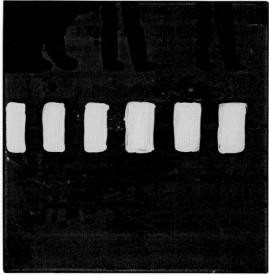

Neil Jeffries
County Fair
Oil on metal
H 59 cm

Frank Bowling OBE RA
And Iona's Green
Acrylic
30 × 25 cm

Diana Armfield RA
*Golden Afternoon in the
Rhyd Yr Efail Fields*
Oil
27 × 29 cm

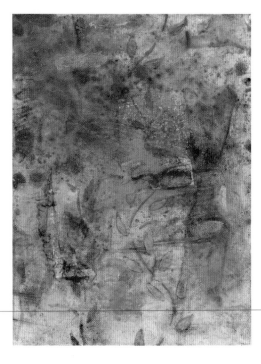

Farah Syed
Real Ghosts
Oil
60 × 70 cm

Jeffery Camp RA
Rose Bud
Oil
30 × 30 cm

Allen Jones RA
Chance of a Lifetime
Oil
30 × 36 cm

Natasha Kidd
Inflate II
Mixed media
51 × 51 cm

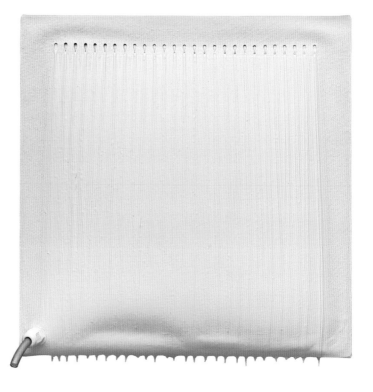

David Batchelor
28.03.11
Mixed media
79 × 61 cm

Anthony Whishaw RA
Light Interior
Acrylic
75 × 75 cm

Taraneh Hemami
Recounting, No. 1
Mixed media
18 × 18 cm

Nadia Hebson
LH
Oil on zinc
45 × 34 cm

Paul Becker
Buttocks Vase
Oil on zinc
29 × 24 cm

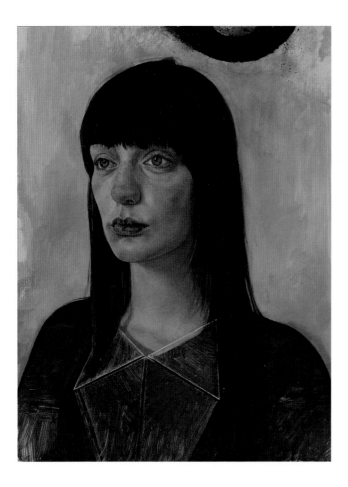

Anthony Green RA
*Aldeburgh II – The Artist at
the South Lookout*
Oil
51 × 87 cm

Timothy Hyman RA
Picturesque Bathroom, Ratisbon
Oil
35 × 52 cm

David Remfry MBE RA
Milonga
Oil
51 × 51 cm

William Bowyer RA
Promising Day
Oil
34 × 47 cm

Sarah Bridgland
Songbirds
Mixed media
9 × 9 cm

Brigitte Williams
Homage to Boetti
Giclée print
H 50 cm

Alison Turnbull
Jefferson (Orange)
Acrylic
107 × 71 cm

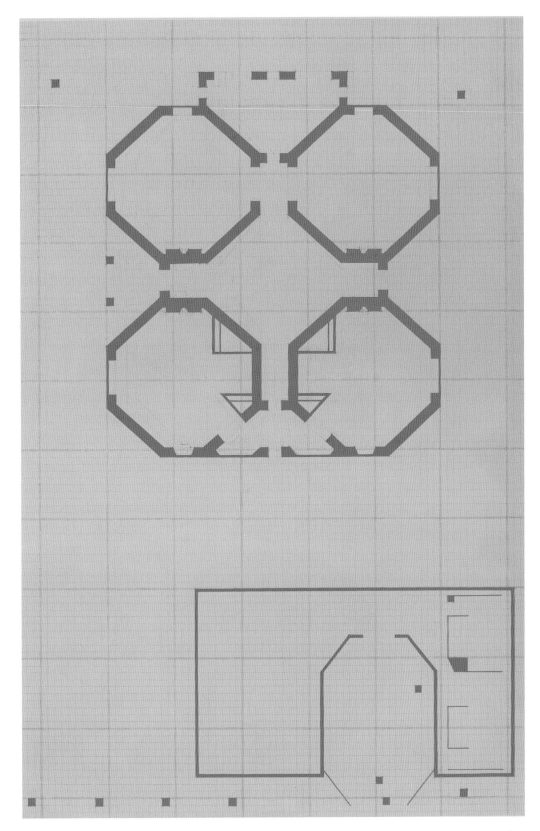

Peter Kalkhof
Colour and Space
Acrylic
30 × 30 cm

Liz Rideal
Echo (Forbes Watson)
Mixed media
Each 26 × 29 cm

Andrew Stahl
Fish Fountain
Oil
35 × 45 cm

Albert Irvin RA
Beta
Acrylic
23 × 17 cm

Alaleh Alamir
Cypress Tree
Etching
98 × 64 cm

Jim Hobbs
Kilnsea: In Obsolescence
Mixed media
12 × 22 cm

Joanna Ciechanowska
E-Migration. Will I Make It?
Mixed media
46 × 80 cm

Alexander Korzer-Robinson
Larousse
Mixed media
33 × 24 cm

Prof Chris Orr MBE RA
Comedy
Etching
59 × 43 cm

Tony Bevan RA
Head
Etching
60 × 45 cm

Michael Craig-Martin CBE RA
Study for Globe 2
Inkjet print
78 × 64 cm

Sir Nicholas Grimshaw CBE PPRA
Cloudy Island
Etching
37 × 27 cm

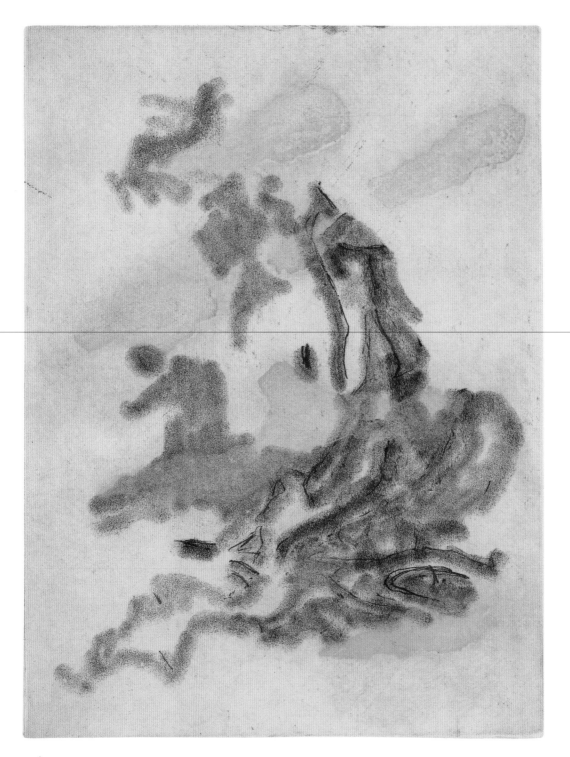

Edward Cullinan CBE RA
Fantastically Flexible Fenestration
Ink
20 × 60 cm

Prof Norman Ackroyd CBE RA
Roareim – Flannan
Etching
15 × 33 cm

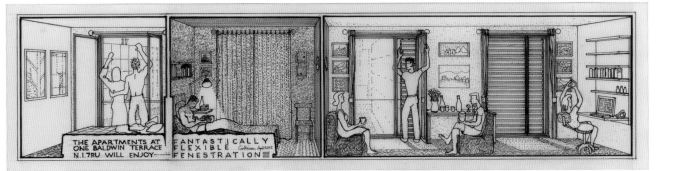

Dr Barbara Rae CBE RA
Yesnaby
Collagraph and etching
55 × 65 cm

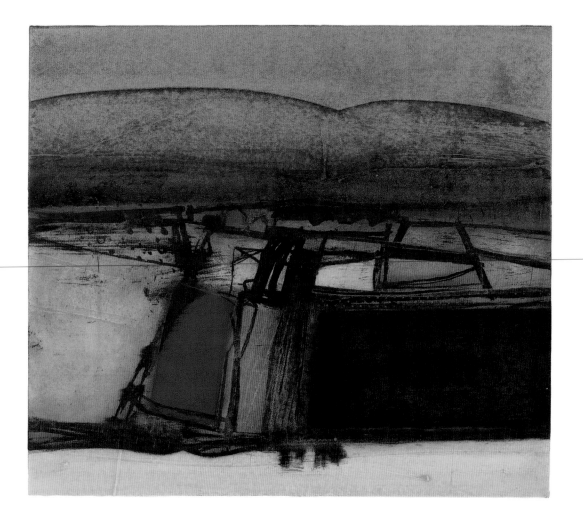

Gillian Ayres CBE RA
Mirabell
Woodcut
75 × 89 cm

Dr Jennifer Dickson RA
Homage to Russell Page (Longleat)
Mixed media
21 × 29 cm

Hughie O'Donoghue RA
Verdant Field I
Carborundum print
48 × 60 cm

Eileen Cooper RA
Blue Boy
Monoprint
77 × 52 cm

Jasia Szerszynska
Seventh Encounter I
Lithograph
48 × 48 cm

Martin Langford
Tunnel Vision
Etching
80 × 138 cm

Anne Desmet RA
London Olympic Velodrome
Wood engraving
10 × 15 cm

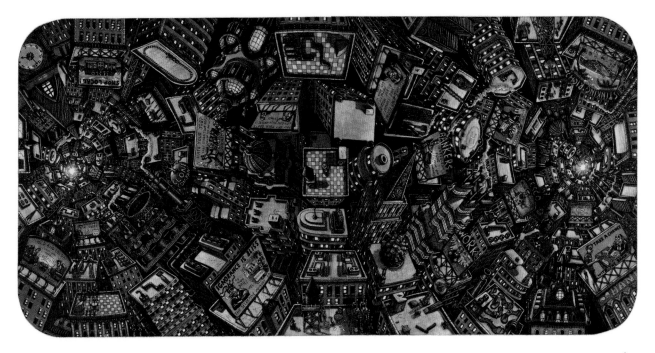

David Borrington
*And Did those Feet in Ancient
Time, London 2012*
Etching
32 × 59 cm

Martin Ridgwell
The Predators
Aquatint
9 × 10 cm

Tamsin Relly
Choppers
Etching
9 × 15 cm

Peter Freeth RA
Coketown, November
Aquatint
10 × 13 cm

Prof Michael Sandle RA
Time of Identity (II)
Aquatint
44 × 60 cm

Rebecca Coleman
On Time
Wood engraving
5 × 5 cm

Katherine Jones
Blue Tile
Etching and block print
55 × 55 cm

Dr Leonard McComb RA
Oranges from the South
Inkjet print
76 × 83 cm

John Carter RA
Unfolding Planes in Yellow
Mixed media
50 × 39 cm

Vanessa Jackson
On Line VIII
Etching
53 × 44 cm

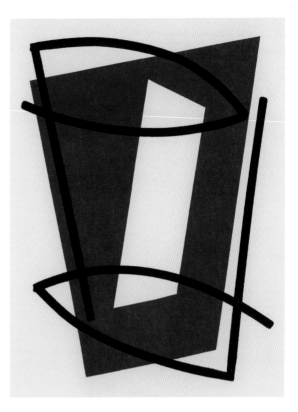

Anselm Kiefer Hon RA
Samson
Mixed media
190 × 380 cm

Gillian Wearing OBE RA
Self-portrait as Woman with Bandaged Face (detail)
C-type print
29 × 95 cm

Humphrey Ocean RA
Shed
Acrylic
70 × 93 cm

Jane Bustin
Tabitha II
Mixed media
35 × 28 cm

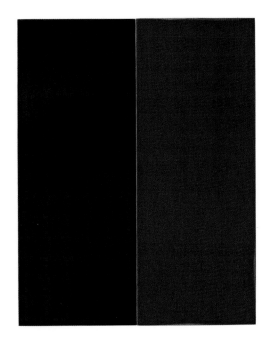

Cornelia Parker OBE RA
Brontëan Abstractions
(Deletions from the Original
Manuscript of 'Jane Eyre')
C-type colour prints
Overall 158 × 158 cm

Onya McCausland
Red with Shadow
Mixed media
165 × 165 cm

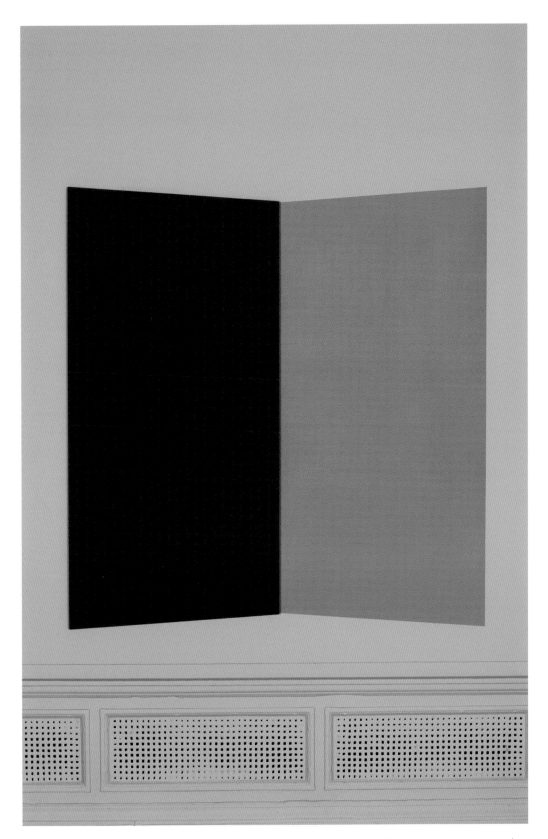

Patrick George
Two Poplars
Oil
114 × 152 cm

Olu Shobowale
Chicken Chair
Chicken bones
H 200 cm

Cathy de Monchaux
Sweetly the Air Flew Overhead, Battle with the Unicorns No. 11
Mixed media
65 × 220 cm

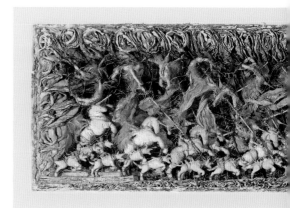

Tomma Abts
Untitled 5
Pencil and coloured pencil
82 × 58 cm

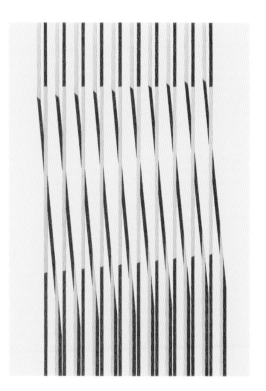

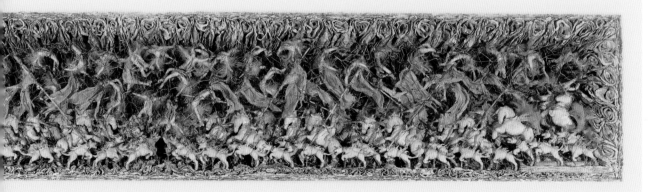

Small
Weston
Room

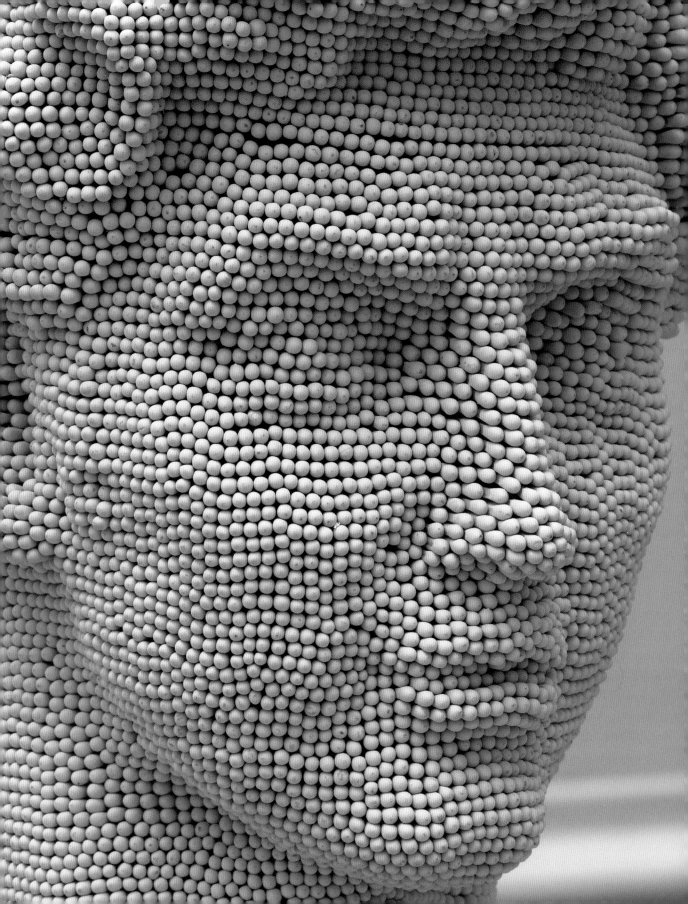

Callum Innes
Untitled No. 33
Oil
196 × 196 cm

Prof Ian Ritchie CBE RA
Turvill's Fountain Close-up
Etching
24 × 24 cm

Sean Scully
Doric Grey
Oil
70 × 92 cm

Jock McFadyen
Buffalo Grill
Oil
172 × 259 cm

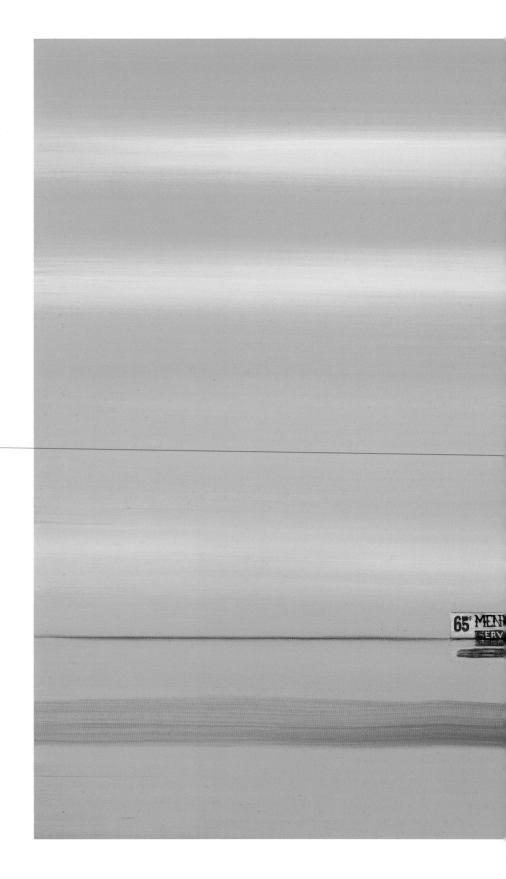

Prof Bryan Kneale RA
Shadow
Enamelled stainless steel
H 65 cm

Scott Mead
Choices
Digital print
151 × 121 cm

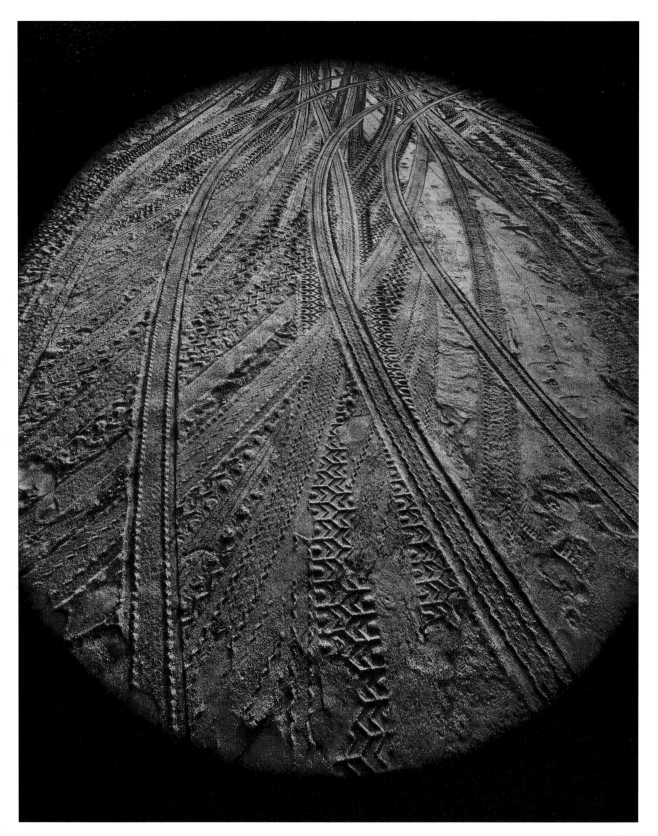

Prof William Alsop OBE RA
A School of Architecture
Acrylic
190 × 350 cm

Graham Crowley
Red Drift, No. 3
Oil
91 × 141 cm

Tom Phillips CBE RA
The Seven Ages of Man
Shaved tennis balls with the artist's hair
H 8 cm

Helena Ben-Zenou
Modern Disco (Cha, Cha, Cha) No.3
Mixed media
76 × 76 cm

Stanton Williams

Creative Spaces: Central Saint Martins at the
New University of the Arts London Campus
Giclée print
152 × 157 cm

Prof Sir Peter Cook RA
Taiwan Tower 3
Digital print
122 × 100 cm

Prof Sir David Chipperfield CBE RA
Turner Contemporary: External Review
Photograph
126 × 163 cm

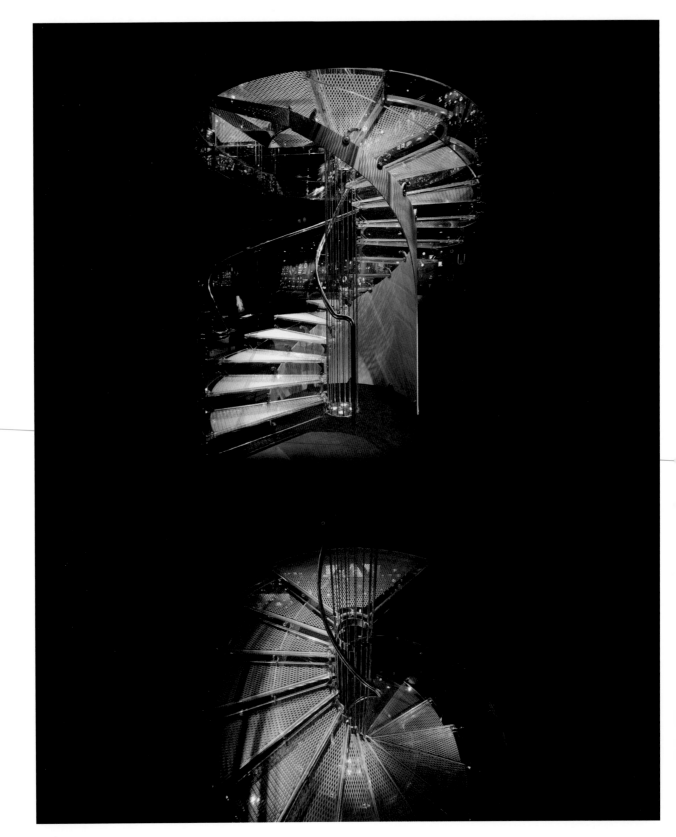

Eva Jiricna CBE RA
Playing with Glass
Duratrans on lightbox
84 × 60 cm

Chris Wilkinson OBE RA
From Landscape to Portrait
Model
H 28 cm

Paul Koralek CBE RA
Concept Sketch – Sheffield
Ink
25 × 33 cm

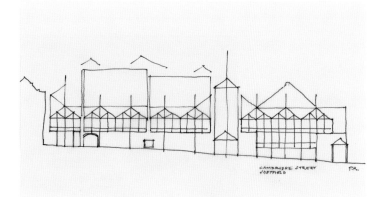

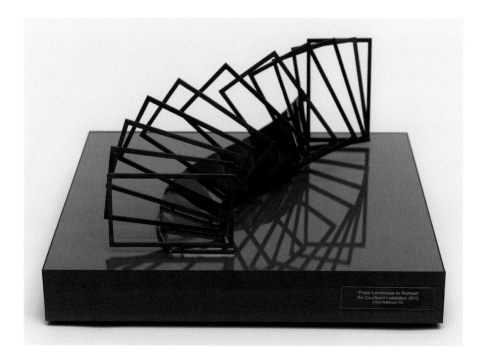

Piers Gough CBE RA
Canada Water Library
Film still

Zaha Hadid CBE RA
Heydar Aliyev Centre, Silver Painting
Mixed media
91 × 200 cm

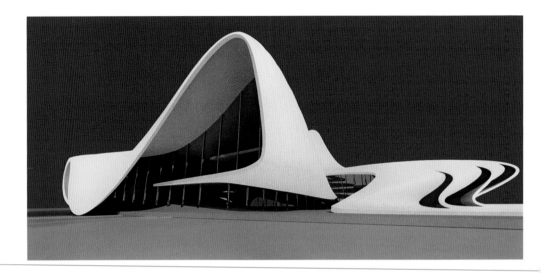

Sir Michael Hopkins CBE RA (Hopkins Architects)
London 2012 Velodrome
Print
54 × 240 cm

Prof Gordon Benson OBE RA
Cityscape
Laserprint
120 × 85 cm

Leonard Manasseh OBE RA
Fly Past
Watercolour
23 × 28 cm

Michael Manser CBE RA
Façade Study, Windowless Hotel
Inkjet print
84 × 60 cm

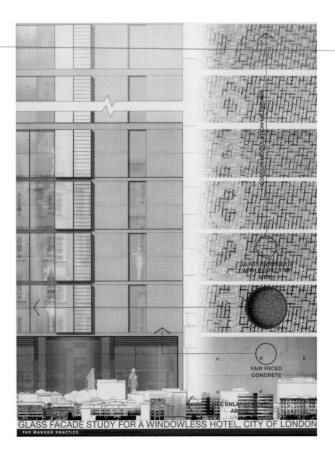

Lord Rogers of Riverside CH RA
Double Core, Scale 1:2000 Hong Kong
Model
H 9 cm

CJ Lim
Dream Isle: London, the Victorian Sponge Cake
Model
H 35 cm

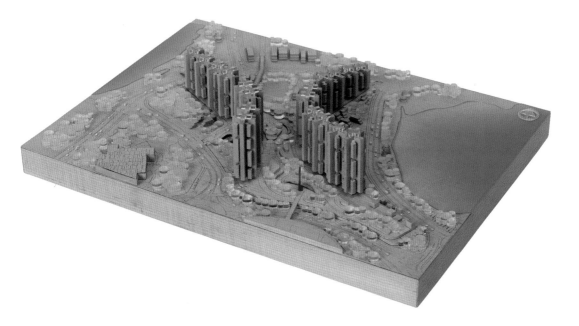

Lord Foster of Thames Bank OM RA
Bloomberg Place, London, Study Sketches (detail)
Pen and pencil
239 × 85 cm

Spencer de Grey CBE RA
Centro Artístico Carlos Acosta, Cuba (detail)
Digital print
120 × 84 cm

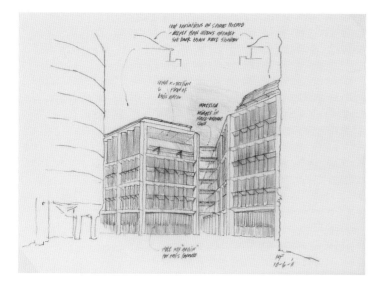

Eric Parry RA
Design Study
Pen and ink wash
27 × 41 cm

Richard Deacon CBE RA
Cornice Proposal, Piccadilly
Model
H 8 cm

Prof Trevor Dannatt RA
Greenford Hall, London Borough of Ealing: Perspectives of Forecourt, Day and Night
Photocollage
41 × 40 cm

Christopher Le Brun PRA
Bell
Patinated bronze
H 31 cm

Phyllida Barlow RA
Untitled: toppledobject
Mixed media
H 179 cm

Also illustrated:

Jill Desborough (left)
The Lovely Rats
Mixed media
H 32 cm

Rachel Alliston (right)
Krampus
Leather
H 179 cm

Prof David Mach RA
Spike
Coathangers
H 122 cm

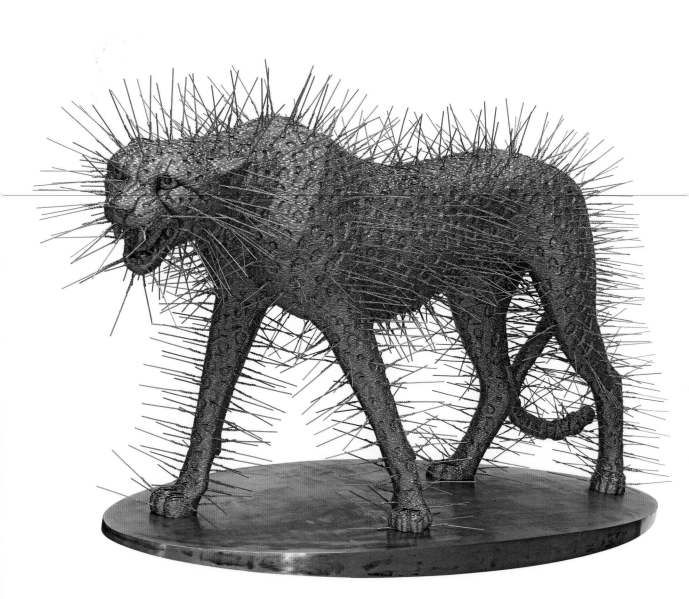

Ana Genovés
Grossular
Mixed media
H 25 cm

James Butler MBE RA
Oracle
Bronze
H 52 cm

Anna Barlow
Miss Sugar Cone Unsure
Ceramic
H 36 cm

Ritva Roesler
Organ I
Felted wool
H 64 cm

Eloise Hawser
Untitled
Mixed media
84 × 84 cm; h 16 cm

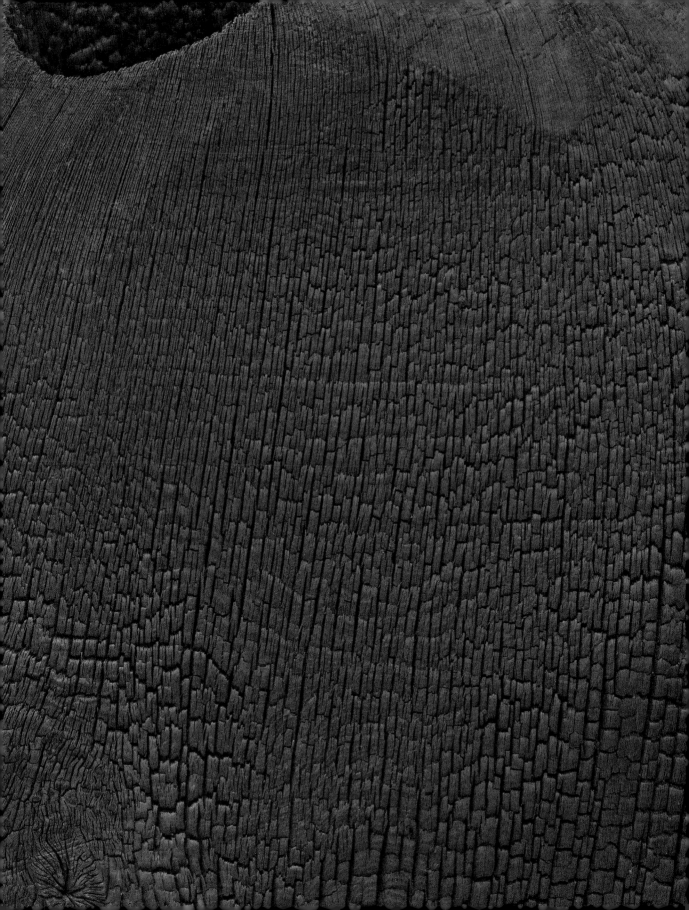

William Sweetlove
Two Cloned Marmots
Silver-plated bronze
H 38 cm

Max Kimber
Long and Long (Before that Time)
Bronze
H 46 cm

Stefania Batoeva
Give and Take
Mixed media
H 25 cm

David Nash OBE RA
Hump with a Hole
Charred oak
H 110 cm

Geoffrey Clarke RA
Flying Boat II
Aluminium
H 7 cm

Ralph Brown RA
Bride
Bronze
H 144 cm

Lucy Glendinning
Feather Child 1
Mixed media
H 23 cm

Kenneth Draper RA
Desert Spirit
Pastel
50 × 45 cm

William Tucker RA
Study for 'Tauromachy'
Charcoal
113 × 127 cm

Stephen Cox RA
Banded Throng
Mixed media
175 × 175 cm

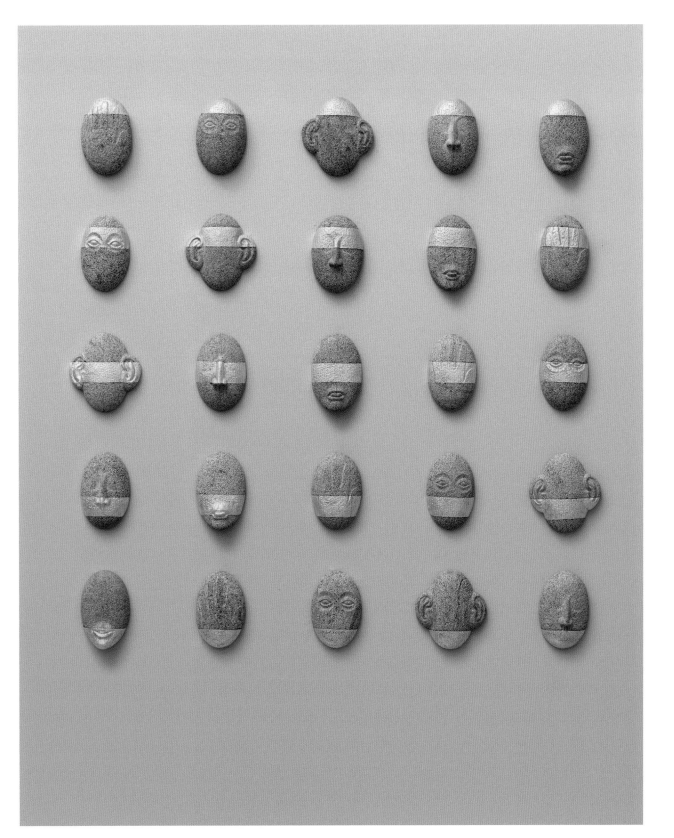

Ann Christopher RA
Silent Space
Mixed media
H 6 cm

Alison Wilding RA
Drone
Mixed media
47 × 61 cm

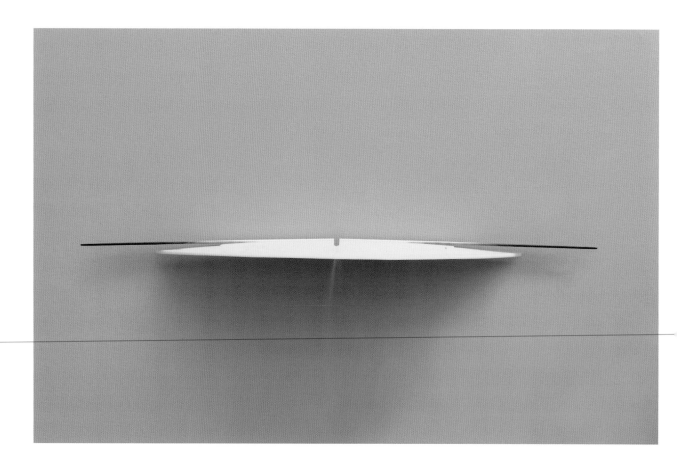

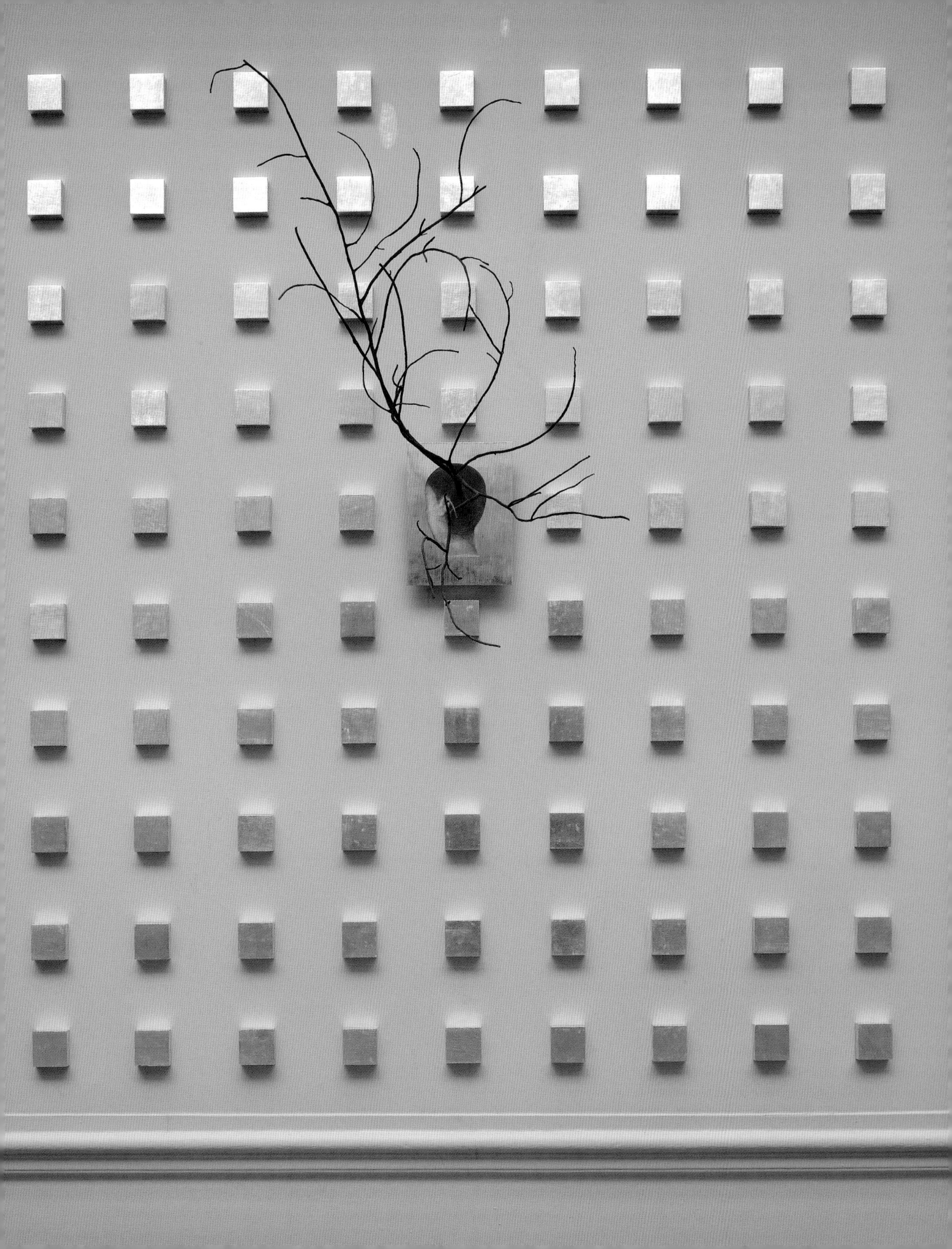

Raqib Shaw
The Last Lament of the First Man of the Universe
Mixed media
H 118 cm

Nigel Hall RA
Southern Shade 1
Polished MDF
H 235 cm

Stephen Chambers RA
I Know Trouble (And She's My Friend)
Oil
150 × 178 cm

Keith Coventry
Junk III
Oil
148 × 122 cm

Lecture
Room

Frederick Cuming Hon DLitt RA
The Wave
Oil
89 × 89 cm

Ken Howard OBE RA
Newlyn Fish Market
Oil
100 × 120 cm

Prof Paul Huxley RA
Proteus XIV
Acrylic
150 × 150 cm

Lisa Milroy RA
Wearable Painting
Mixed media
H 150 cm

Mick Moon RA
Redwoods
Acrylic
122 × 122 cm

David Austen
Pink Tree
Oil
198 × 183 cm

Humphrey Ocean RA
Surface
Oil
126 × 178 cm

Prof Ian McKeever RA
Twelve/Standing
Oil and acrylic
270 × 190 cm

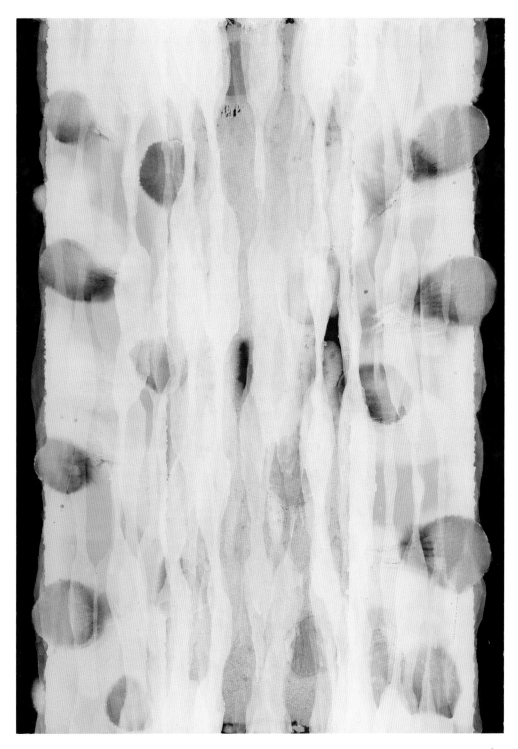

John Maine RA
Mitre
Swedish granite
H 69 cm

Jennifer Durrant RA
Series 'Ghirlanda continua': Italia No. 23
Acrylic
98 × 98 cm

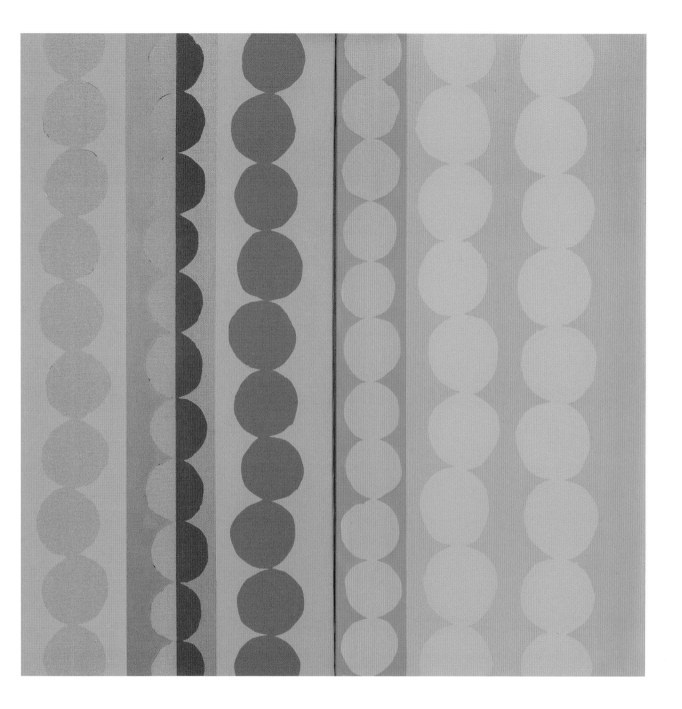

Terry Setch RA
Remembering Chernobyl
Mixed media
168 × 210 cm

Fathi Hassan
Butterfly
Mixed media
138 × 98 cm

Prof Phillip King CBE PPRA
Ring Reel Maquette
Steel, from PUC
H 26 cm

Prof Dhruva Mistry CBE RA
Recline
Mixed media
H 40 cm

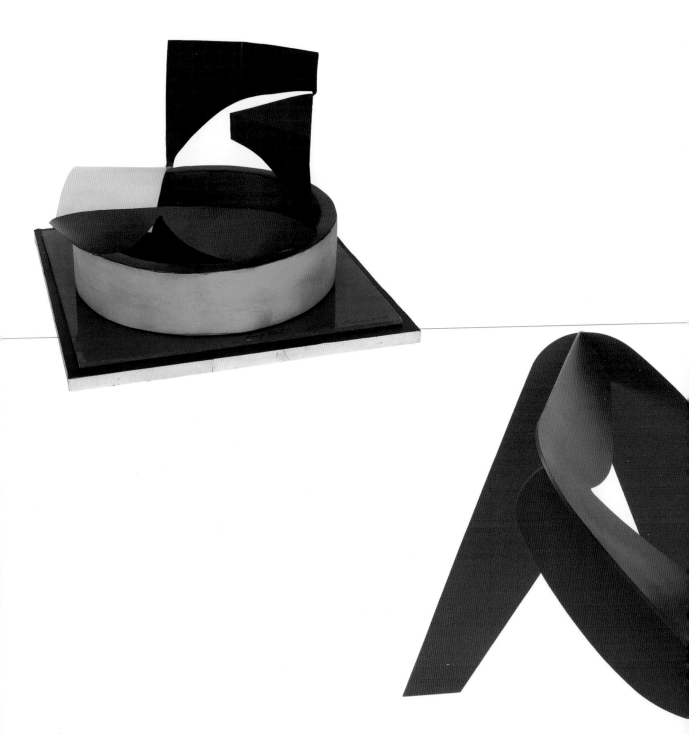

Prof Maurice Cockrill RA
Dancing around Midnight
Acrylic
200 × 249 cm

Joe Tilson RA
Finestra Veneziana Venessia 3
Mixed media
100 × 105 cm

Philip Sutton RA
A Fairy Tale in a Forest
Oil
183 × 121 cm

Prof Ivor Abrahams RA
Flower Bed
Mixed media
67 × 97 cm

Christian Junghanns
Couple Orange
Acrylic
85 × 120 cm

Sir Anthony Caro OM CBE RA
Reliquary House
Mixed media
H 30 cm

Anthony Eyton RA
Tapestry
Oil
110 × 78 cm

Prof Richard Wilson RA
Hang on a minute lads, I've got a great idea…
Mixed media
41 × 59 cm

Stuart Dawson
Composition with Mars and Ivory Black
Mixed media
40 × 47 cm

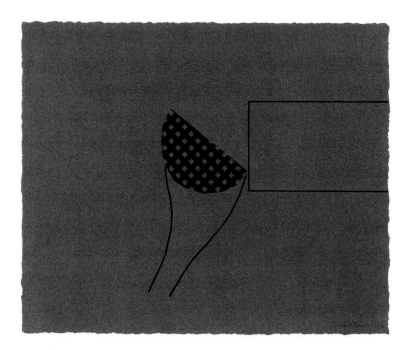

Thomas Nozkowski
Untitled (8-129)
Mixed media
56 × 71 cm

Zachary Beer
Imp Metabolic Pathway: Step 1
Oil
47 × 51 cm

Prof Tracey Emin RA
Upset
Acrylic
185 × 185 cm

Georg Baselitz Hon RA
Frau Manets Rechter Fuß
Oil
208 × 155 cm

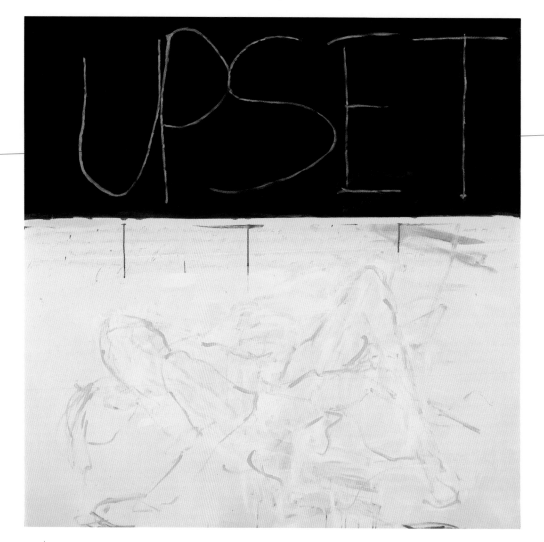

James Fisher
Migraine Weather
Oil
55 × 60 cm

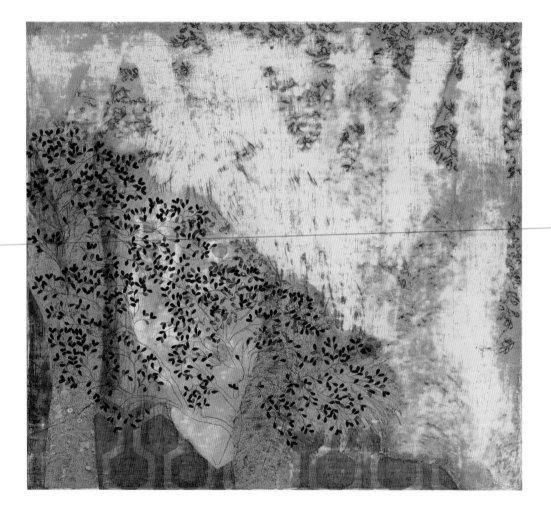

Bill Jacklin RA
Battery Park Under the Tree, NYC 1
Oil
170 × 153 cm

Gary Hume RA
The Field
Gloss on aluminium
140 × 240 cm

Martin Creed
Work No. 623
Green neon
H 15 cm

Prof Fiona Rae RA
Untitled (Small Collage No. 26)
Mixed media
19 × 15 cm

Dexter Dalwood
Stevie
Oil
150 × 135 cm

Index

Royal Academy of Arts in London, 2012

Registered charity number 1125383

Officers

President
Christopher Le Brun PRA

Keeper
Eileen Cooper RA
Treasurer
Prof Paul Huxley RA

Secretary and Chief Executive
Dr Charles Saumarez Smith CBE

Past Presidents

Sir Philip Dowson CBE PPRA

Sir Nicholas Grimshaw CBE PPRA

Prof Phillip King CBE PPRA

Senior Academicians

Prof Ivor Abrahams
Diana Armfield
Gillian Ayres CBE
Basil Beattie
Dame Elizabeth Blackadder DBE
Sir Peter Blake CBE
Olwyn Bowey
Frank Bowling OBE
William Bowyer
Ralph Brown
James Butler MBE
Jeffery Camp
Sir Anthony Caro OM CBE
Geoffrey Clarke

Robert Clatworthy
Edward Cullinan CBE
Frederick Cuming HON DLITT
Prof Trevor Dannatt
Sir Philip Dowson CBE PPRA
Bernard Dunstan
Anthony Eyton
Mary Fedden OBE
Lord Foster of Thames Bank OM
Sir Michael Hopkins CBE
Ken Howard OBE
Albert Irvin
Prof Phillip King CBE PPRA
Prof Bryan Kneale

Paul Koralek CBE
Sonia Lawson
Dr Leonard McComb
Leonard Manasseh OBE
Michael Manser CBE
John Partridge CBE
Lord Rogers of Riverside CH
Prof Michael Sandle
Terry Setch
Philip Sutton
Joe Tilson
Dr David Tindle
William Tucker
Anthony Whishaw

Academicians

Prof Norman Ackroyd CBE
Prof William Alsop OBE
Phyllida Barlow
Dr John Bellany CBE
Prof Gordon Benson OBE
Tony Bevan
John Carter
*Stephen Chambers
Prof Sir David Chipperfield CBE
Ann Christopher
Dr Jennifer Dickson
Kenneth Draper
Jennifer Durrant
Prof Tracey Emin
Prof Stephen Farthing
*Peter Freeth
Antony Gormley OBE
Piers Gough CBE
Anthony Green
Spencer de Grey CBE
Sir Nicholas Grimshaw CBE PPRA
Zaha Hadid CBE
Nigel Hall
David Hockney OM CH
Gary Hume
Prof Paul Huxley

Timothy Hyman
Bill Jacklin
*Tess Jaray
*Eva Jiricna CBE
Allen Jones
Anish Kapoor CBE
Michael Landy
Christopher Le Brun PRA
Richard Long
Sir Richard MacCormac CBE
Prof David Mach
Prof Ian McKeever
John Maine
Lisa Milroy
Prof Dhruva Mistry CBE
Mick Moon
Mali Morris
David Nash OBE
*Humphrey Ocean
Hughie O'Donoghue
*Prof Chris Orr MBE
Cornelia Parker OBE
Eric Parry
Grayson Perry
Tom Phillips CBE
*Dr Barbara Rae CBE

Prof Fiona Rae
David Remfry MBE
Prof Ian Ritchie CBE
Mick Rooney
Jenny Saville
Alan Stanton
Gillian Wearing OBE
*Alison Wilding
*Chris Wilkinson OBE
Prof Richard Wilson
Bill Woodrow
John Wragg

*Hanging Committee 2012

Honorary Academicians

Marina Abramovic
Tadao Ando
Georg Baselitz
Frank O Gehry
Rebecca Horn
Arata Isozaki
Jasper Johns
Ellsworth Kelly

Anselm Kiefer
Per Kirkeby
Jeff Koons
Daniel Libeskind
Bruce Nauman
Mimmo Paladino
Ieoh Ming Pei
Renzo Piano

Ed Ruscha
Julian Schnabel
Richard Serra
Cindy Sherman
Frank Stella
James Turrell
Ai Weiwei

Royal Academy of Arts

The Royal Academy of Arts has a unique position as an independent institution led by eminent artists and architects whose purpose is to promote the creation, enjoyment and appreciation of the visual arts through exhibitions, education and debate. The Royal Academy receives no annual funding via government, and is entirely reliant on self-generated income and charitable support.

You and/or your company can support the Royal Academy of Arts in a number of different ways:

- Almost £60 million has been raised for capital projects, including the Jill and Arthur M Sackler Wing, the restoration of the Main Galleries, the restoration of the John Madejski Fine Rooms, and the provision of better facilities for the display and enjoyment of the Academy's own collections of important works of art and documents charting the history of British art.
- Donations from individuals, trusts, companies and foundations also help support the Academy's internationally renowned exhibition programme, the conservation of the Collections and education projects for schools, families and people with special needs; as well as providing scholarships and bursaries for postgraduate art students in the Royal Academy Schools.
- As a company, you can invest in the Royal Academy through arts sponsorship, corporate membership and corporate entertaining, with specific opportunities that relate to your budgets and marketing or entertaining objectives.

- If you would like to preserve the Academy for future generations, please consider remembering us in your will. Your gift can be a sum of money, a specific item or a share of what is left after you have provided for your family and friends. Any gift, large or small, could help ensure that our work continues in the future.

To find out ways in which individuals can support this work, or a specific aspect of it, please contact Charlotte Appleyard, Head of Patrons, on 020 7300 5977.

To explore ways in which companies, trusts and foundations can become involved in the work of the Academy, please contact the Project Giving Office on 020 7300 5629/5979.

For more information on remembering the Academy in your will, please contact Emma Warren-Thomas on 020 7300 5677 or legacies@royalacademy.org.uk

Membership of the Friends

The Friends of the Royal Academy was founded in 1977 to support and promote the work of the Royal Academy. It is now one of the largest such organisations in the world, with around 90,000 members.

As a Friend you enjoy free entry to every RA exhibition and much more...

- Invites to Preview Days before exhibitions open to the public
- Bring one adult family guest and up to four family children under 16 to any exhibition for free
- Use of the Friends Room

- Receive the quarterly *RA Magazine*
- Access to a programme of Friends events
- Keep up to date with the Friends e-news, packed with events, news and offers

Why not join today?

- At the Friends desk in the Front Hall
- Online at www.royalacademy.org.uk/friends

- Ring 020 7300 5664 any day of the week
- E-mail friends.enquiries@royalacademy.org.uk

Summer Exhibition Organisers

Natalie Bouloudis
Edith Devaney
Lorna Burn
Josephine New
Katherine Oliver
Jessica Parry
Paul Sirr
Jessica Smith

Royal Academy Publications

Beatrice Gullström
Elizabeth Horne
Carola Krueger
Sophie Oliver
Peter Sawbridge
Nick Tite

Book design: Adam Brown_01.02
Photography: John Bodkin, DawkinsColour
Colour reproduction: DawkinsColour
Printed in Italy by Graphicom

British Library
Cataloguing-in-publication Data
A catalogue record for this book
is available in the British Library

ISBN 978-1-907533-14-3

Acknowledgements

The extract from Wallace Stevens's
poem 'The Man with the Blue Guitar'
on page 16 is printed by kind permission
of Faber & Faber.

Illustrations

Page 2: Gillian Ayres CBE RA, *Mirabell*
(detail)
Page 4: Tess Jaray RA, *After Malevich*
(detail)
Pages 6, 23: the Wohl Central Hall with
Dr Leonard McComb RA's *Portrait
of a Young Man Standing*
Pages 10–11: members of the 2012
Hanging Committee, from left,
Humphrey Ocean RA, Prof Chris
Orr MBE RA, Tess Jaray RA, Peter
Freeth RA
Pages 14–15: installation view of Gallery
III
Page 29: Frank Bowling OBE RA,
And Iona's Green (detail)
Pages 40–41: installation view of Gallery
III
Page 63: Alexander Korzer-Robinson,
Larousse (detail)
Page 75: Hughie O'Donoghue RA,
Verdant Field I (detail)
Page 81: installation view of Gallery I
Page 87: installation view of the Large
Weston Room with Paul de
Monchaux's *Arc* and *Sea Lily*
Page 99: Jayne Parker, *Self-portrait 2*
Page 101: Prof David Mach RA, *David
(No. 9 of 8)* (detail)
Page 107: Graham Crowley, *Red Drift,
No. 3* (detail)
Page 113: Rana Begum, *No. 283*
Page 125: Prof David Mach RA, *Spike*
(detail)
Page 133: David Nash OBE RA, *Hump
with a Hole* (detail)
Pages 138–39: installation view of
Gallery VIII, with Bill Woodrow
RA's *Illuminator A* and *Illuminator B*
Page 147: Mimmo Palladino HON RA,
Untitled
Page 153: Joe Tilson RA, *Finestra
Veneziana Venessia 3* (detail)
Pages 154–55: installation view of the
Lecture Room
Page 179: James Fisher, *Migraine Weather*
(detail)

Photographic Acknowledgements

Pages 8, 10–11, 12–13: Phil Sayer
Page 16: © the Estate of Leonard
Rosoman
Page 17: © National Portrait Gallery,
London
Page 27: the artist, courtesy Waddington
Custot Galleries
Page 34 (top): courtesy the artist and
Hauser & Wirth
Page 39 (bottom): courtesy Purdy Hicks
Gallery
Page 43 (top): courtesy Galerie Nikki
Diana Marquardt, Paris
Page 48 (bottom): courtesy the artist and
Wilkinson Gallery
Page 53: courtesy the artist
Page 59: courtesy the artist and Matt's
Gallery, London
Page 60 (top): © Peter Kalkhof, courtesy
Annely Juda Fine Art
Pages 88–89: © the artist, courtesy White
Cube
Pages 94–95: courtesy Browse & Darby
Ltd
Page 97 (top): courtesy greengrassi,
London
Page 102: courtesy the artist and Frith
Street Gallery, London
Page 103 (top): © the artist, courtesy
Timothy Taylor Gallery
Page 113: courtesy BISCHOFF/WEISS,
London
Page 115: Simon Menges
Page 116: Katsuhisa Kida
Page 118 (bottom): © Andrew
Unterhalter and Hopkins
Architects
Page 122 (top): Foster + Partners
Page 148: © the artist, courtesy White
Cube
Page 151: courtesy the artist and The
Pace Gallery
Page 177 (bottom): © Thomas
Nozkowski, courtesy The Pace
Gallery
Page 182: © Tracey Emin. All rights
reserved, DACS 2012
Page 183: © Georg Baselitz, photo
Jochen Littkemann, Berlin
Page 185: courtesy the artist and Hauser
& Wirth, © Hugo Glendinning
Page 187: © 2012 Dexter Dalwood,
courtesy Gagosian Gallery

Large
Weston
Room